HOW TO MAKE SALES TO MULTIPLY YOUR INCOME;

Steps To Bring In More Sales To Your Business

Jin McKenzie

Table of content

Introduction

There is definitely not an enchanted equation which prompts sales achievement. Fortunately various standards and steps will assist you with forming into an effective dealer on the off chance that you follow them. A great many people can secure, and use, the abilities expected to sell.

NOTABLE QUOTES BY SALES SPECIALISTS.........

"A brand for a company is like a reputation for a person. You earn a reputation by trying to do hard things well."
   Jeff Bezos

"If you double the number of experiments you do per year you're going to double your inventiveness."
   Jeff Bezos

"Setting goals is the first step in turning the invisible into the visible."

Tony Robbins

Every time you state what you want or believe, you're the first to hear it. It's a message to both you and others about what you think is possible. Don't put a ceiling on yourself."

- Oprah Winfrey

"It's fine to celebrate success but it is more important to heed the lessons of failure."

- Bill Gates

"I have not failed. I've just found 10,000 ways that won't work."

- Thomas Edison

"As long as you're going to be thinking anyway, think big."

- Donald Trump

"Success is walking from failure to failure with no loss of enthusiasm."

- Winston Churchill

"Genius is 1% inspiration, and 99% perspiration."

- Thomas Edison

"Twenty years from now you will be more disappointed by the things that you didn't do than by the ones you did do. So throw off the bowlines. Sail away from the safe harbor. Catch the trade winds in your sails. Explore. Dream. Discover."

- *Mark Twain*

"Keep away from people who try to belittle your ambitions. Small people always do that, but the really great ones make you feel that you, too, can become great."
Mark Twain
"If you don't find a way to make money while you sleep, you will work until you die."

Warren Buffett

What differentiates sellers today is their ability to bring fresh ideas.
Jill Konrath

Chapter 1

What Do You Mean By "Sales"

By definition, the expression "sales" alludes to movements of every sort engaged with offering an item or administration to a purchaser or business. However, by and by, it implies a lot more.

A ton of exertion goes into effectively settling a negotiation - from obtaining possibilities, to building connections, and giving clients arrangements. We'll dive into sorts of deals, normal deals terms, and deals systems to assist you with tackling for the client and increment income.

WHAT ARE SALES?

Sales is a term used to portray the exercises that lead to the selling of labor and products. Organizations have sales with associations that are separated into various groups. Also, these outreach groups are in many cases decided in light of the locale they're offering to, the item or administration they're selling, and the objective client.

Sales can be supposed to be between at least two gatherings in which the purchaser gets products, administrations and resources in return for cash. Sales happens when cash is traded for responsibility for an item or administration.

Organizations staff whole offices with representatives devoted to selling their items and administrations. Salesmen connect with contacts that may be keen on buying the item or administration that their organization is selling — possibilities that show interest through activities like visiting the organization site or associating with the organization via web-based entertainment.

The objective is to contact leads who have shown interest in or fit the depiction of the organization's objective client, in order to give them an answer that outcomes in an acquisition of your item or administration.

While numerous outreach groups are held to month to month quantities and benchmarks for changing over leads and finishing up with, the genuine objective of deals is addressing for the client.

Promoting And Sales

Where could sales reps at any point source leads and prospects? The missions and endeavors of the showcasing association are the absolute most ideal ways to produce qualified leads. Also, the State of Inbound Report found that sales reps source 28% of their leads from promoting. While advertising and deals utilize various cycles, both business capabilities influence lead age and income.

All in all, how do outreach groups sell? We should survey the most widely recognized sorts of deals.

Types of Sales

Inside Sales
Outside Sales
B2B Sales
B2C Sales
Business Development Sales
Office Sales
Consultative sales
Online business sales
Direct sales
Account based sales.

1. Inside Sales
At the point when outreach groups draw in with their possibilities and clients from a distance, frequently from an office close to their colleagues, they follow an inside deals approach. This implies they are selling from inside their

organization. Associations that utilize an inside deals approach frequently will quite often have less fatty, more robotized processes and organized hours.

Inside Sales in real life: AT&T

kinds of deals model inside deals

From telephone administration to web to TV, AT&T gives items and administrations to pretty much any shopper and business. The organization's inside agents contact leads and prospects to finish the customary deals process — uncovering the clients' necessities, coordinating them with the right arrangement, and settling the negotiation. They could utilize business programming to monitor client corporations and deals won.

2. Outside Sales

In groups where sales reps represent up close and personal arrangements with the possibility, they are following an external deals approach.

This suggests that they are selling from outside their organization — customarily through house to house or handling deals. These groups tend to not have rigorously controlled processes, permitting opportunity and adaptability for reps to create and execute their own deals methodologies.

Outside Sales in real life: Medtronic

As a forerunner in clinical grade hardware, Medtronic uses the range of abilities of experienced salesmen to coordinate their items with clinical experts. Clinical gadgets agents invest most of their energy voyaging — yet when they arrive at their objections, they meet with clinical experts and overseers who come to conclusions about what to buy.

As well as venturing out to imminent clients, they could go to meetings and occasions where these chiefs may be to organize and fabricate connections before now is the ideal time to make a deal.

3. B2B Sales

This normal abbreviation means "business-to-business" and depicts organizations that offer items and administrations to different organizations, rather than individual shoppers.

B2B deals will quite often have a higher ticket worth and more mind boggling terms on the grounds that the merchandise offered to different organizations commonly assume a fundamental part in how the purchaser's business works.

Inside the domain of B2B, dealers can fundamentally uphold SMBs (little to medium organizations) or undertaking clients.

B2B Sales in real life: GetAccept

GetAccept is a deals enablement stage that assists salespeople fabricate associations with purchasers. As a business that assists different organizations with selling better, GetAccept characterizes it as a B2B organization. Its agents work with different outreach group supervisors to advance the advantages of the GetAccept items and make long haul clients that produce income for the business over the long haul.

4. B2C Sales
In contrast to B2B deals, B2C (or business-to-shopper) deals spin around exchanges between an organization and its singular buyers. These arrangements will generally be of lower value worth and intricacy than B2B deals and can include various arrangements with different clients.

B2C Sales in real life: uPacktypes of deals model B2C

Moving organizations depend on B2C deals to associate straightforwardly with the buyer who utilizes their administrations. uPack utilizes advanced advertisements to source leads which their B2C outreach group transforms into clients.

Its deals cycle is straightforward, however successful — the organization gets clients intrigued by their administrations by offering them a free statement on their turn. Then, at that point, the B2C agents get to work tempting the planned client to pick their moving assistance over the opposition in view of lower costs and quicker moves.

5. Business Development Sales
However business improvement doesn't represent a whole deals exchange, it's a significant part of the deals capability for some organizations. This job is regularly held by Slack

kinds of deals model business improvement

BDRs at Slack are liable for the pipeline inside big business accounts. They drive effort to a few partners at the organizations where they work. Individuals in these jobs are supposed to be item specialists and fabricate interest for the Slack item.

6. Organization Sales
This kind of deals includes creating and
changing new leads over completely to sign onto
administration bundles from an organization. As
indicated by HubSpot's 2019 State of Agency
Selling, the typical organization deals cycle is
somewhere in the range of 31 and 90 days, with
most organizations welcoming one to three new
clients every month.

In the office deals space, clients are normally
marked either by project or on a retainer. For
organizations that sign clients by project, they
principally center around acquiring new
business, selling administration bundles to new
clients as their ongoing activities wrap up.

With a retainer model, organizations can draw in
with clients on a continuous premise which
considers unsurprising repeating pay with less
reliance on getting a constant flow of new
clients.

Organization Sales in real life: UMG

The UMG group of siblings began their imaginative organization utilizing organization deals — auctioning one-off projects like strategies and continuous site administrations to organizations in South Carolina. Presently, the business has developed to extravagant levels with a few faithful clients on retainer.

7. Consultative Sales
Consultative selling is a way of selling that spotlights on building entrust with the client to comprehend their requirements prior to suggesting a particular item or administration.

With consultative selling, agents center around building a relationship with the purchaser and driving the deal with how the contribution will help the singular client, rather than exclusively zeroing in on the elements of the item to make the deal.

Consultative Sales in real life: Legacy Home Loans

kinds of deals model consultative deals

While looking for a home loan moneylender, there are a ton of factors that can impact a house purchaser's choice to pick one over the other. Actually, those factors are difficult numbers.

Consultative deals work for contract banks since they can carry a human viewpoint to the home credit process. Inheritance Home Loans does precisely this, in any event, estimating achievement "each grin in turn."

8. Online business Sales
Does your organization sell items solely on the web? Is your client ready to explore your item, decide if they need to get it, and make their buy online all without expecting to draw in with somebody from your organization? Provided that this is true, you're following an eCommerce or online deals model.

However this kind of auctioning is a larger number of hands-off than different sorts, it can function admirably for lean organizations who can't staff a full outreach group, or for organizations who offer items that can be really sold through designated computerized showcasing.

Overall eCommerce deals increased by over 27% in 2020, and Kissed By A Bee got a portion of that development. This organization gives natural cures and magnificence items totally on the web. While it gives live client care, the majority of their promoting and deals endeavors occur totally on the web.

9. Direct Sales

With an immediate selling model, people can sell straightforwardly to shoppers beyond a conventional retail climate. With this technique, dealers direct the deal one-on-one with their clients, frequently procuring a commission. This type of selling is normally utilized by network advertising delegates and realtors.

Direct Sales in real life: Telfar

Telfar is a global gender neutral style organization established in 2005. As a totally computerized business, orders must be put on the web and are not sold in retail chains like customary design brands are. The organization is known to sell out of its purses and frills in minutes which has made a famous recycled retail market for the brand's product.

10. Account Based Sales
Organizations that have enormous endeavor accounts with a few resources hope to account based deals to serve these clients. Not at all like business improvement deals, account based outreach groups don't hand off their chances to a deals improvement rep to close.

All things considered, the open door stays inside the record based group to serve that client from lead to an open door and the entire way through to client achievement. The advantage of record based deals is that the outreach group will construct a relationship with the undertaking over a more extended timeframe which results in a higher LTV.

Account Based Sales in real life: PepsiCo

Could you at any point envision how troublesome it is to purchase your soft drink straightforwardly from the packaging distribution center? In the same way as other food and drink organizations, PepsiCo works with retailers of all sizes, areas, and types to get its items to purchasers.

To deal with all of this, the organization adopts a record based strategy to deals and record the executives. The job answerable for dealing with these connections previously, during, and after the deal is known as the Key Account Manager (KAM).

They're answerable for accomplishing beneficial sales for enormous retail locations like Walmart and Target. KAMs guarantee that the interest from the record matches what the outreach group has gauge for the record so buyers never find a store that is out of Mountain Dew.

Normal Sales Terms

Here are a portion of the normal terms that are related to deals and selling which you want to comprehend.

1. **Sales rep**

A sales rep is a person who plays out every one of the exercises related to selling an item or helping. Equivalent words for sales rep incorporate deals partner, dealer, deals specialist, and agent or delegate.

2. **Prospect**

A possibility is a resource at an organization that the sales rep might want to offer items or administrations to. The sales rep utilizes prospecting procedures like settling on warm decisions, email effort, and social selling. What's more, in the event that they're keen on the item or administration, the salesman can apply various deal-shopping procedures to transform the possibility into a client.

3. Bargain

An arrangement addresses the item or administration you might want to sell and the cost related to it. Bargains have various stages, which can shift contingent upon the business, its cycles, items, and industry — and bargain execution can be followed utilizing a CRM. Sales reps can assemble bargains intended to make the selling system more straightforward on the possibility and the agent.

4. Sales Pipeline

Sales pipeline depicts every one of the means in your deals cycle. It provides sales reps with a visual portrayal of where possibilities are in the deals cycle.

What Is Sales Deal FunnelImage Source

As per the Gartner 2021 Chief Sales Officer survey, the best two needs of deals associations in the U.S. were building another deals pipeline and empowering virtual selling.

5. Sales Plan

The sales plan frames the objectives, goals, and systems for a deals association. It incorporates insights concerning objective clients, economic situations, income targets, evaluating, group construction, from there, the sky's the limit. It likewise spreads out the strategies the outreach groups will use to accomplish their objectives.

Kinds Of Sales Methodologies

A sales interaction is critical to running a fruitful deals association. Here are a portion of the top deals philosophies organizations use.

Arrangement Selling: Solution selling is the point at which the sales rep drives the discussion with the advantages that a custom arrangement will give the possibility. This technique recognizes that possibilities are educated and have investigated as needs be on the item or administration before the agent connects.

Inbound Selling: With this deals strategy, sales reps go about as an expert. They meet the possibilities where they are and tackle for possibilities' trouble spots.

Turn Selling: SPIN is utilized to portray the four kinds of inquiries sales reps ought to pose to their clients: Situation, Problem, Implication, and Need-Payoff. The inquiries recognize the possibility's problem areas and assist the salesman with building affinity with the purchaser.

N.E.A.T. Selling: This is a system that is utilized to qualify leads. N.E.A.T. represents: center necessities, financial effect, admittance to power, and convincing occasion.

Reasonable Selling: Conceptual selling is a technique where salesmen reveal the possibility's idea of their item and try to comprehend the possibility's choice interaction.

SNAP Selling: SNAP selling is an abbreviation for: Keep it Simple, be iNvaluable, consistently Align, and raise Priorities.

The Challenger Sale: The Challenger Sale follows an instruct tailor-take control process. Sales reps show the possibility, tailor their correspondences, and assume command over the deal.

The Sandler System: This framework focuses on building shared trust between the agent and prospect. The sales rep goes about as a counsel and poses inquiries to recognize the possibility's difficulties.

Client Centric Selling: With this strategy, the sales rep centers around speaking with the key chiefs in the deal, and tracking down answers for address their trouble spots or difficulties.

MEDDIC: MEDDIC represents: measurements, financial purchaser, choice rules, choice cycle, distinguish torment, champion. The sales rep poses inquiries about these subjects to assist with moving the possibility to push ahead in the deals cycle.

Get Familiar With The Art Of Sales

The essential objectives of deals are to make custom answers for their possibilities and produce income for the business. Whether you're searching for potential learning experiences inside deals or you're joining the field interestingly, we trust this speedy manual for deals has furnished you with an essential comprehension of the sorts of deals you can do and how they work inside the whole business.

Chapter 2

How to create sales?

To build sales for your business, creating more potential customers is vital. This is the way to create more prospective customers for your business.

Lead age traverses across numerous touch focuses for some organizations. For a business to endure its requirements to create potential customers in the principal case.

What Is A Prospective Customer?

Prospective customers are the existence blood of outreach groups. A lead can be either an individual or organization who you desire to win as a future client for your administration or item.

A potential customer is an individual or business that could buy your organization's labor and products. A lead turns into a possibility whenever you've distinguished their degree of interest and fit as a client for your business. You can utilize various strategies to recognize prospective customers, including promoting and showcasing, cold pitching, online entertainment, references, exceed and systems administration, meetings, and item/administration preliminaries.

What is a warm lead?

This is where an individual or organization has demonstrated interest in your organization's administration or item

What is lead age?

Lead age is the method involved with obtaining prospective customers for example purchasing records. For organizations intensely centered around inbound, it is the making of mindfulness and the inception of an individual or organization's advantage into your organization's item or administration.

Who claims lead age?

In many associations showcasing commonly possesses this. Outreach groups will likewise do their own prospecting by means of the web or different information sources.

There is a timeless conflict among Marketing and Sales in regards to the volume and nature of deals prompts hit deals targets. Where there is a sufficient stock, the world can be agreeable yet in the event that there are issues with lead volume or lead quality you will hear the everlasting words:

Sales: "The leads are low quality and I have need something more"

Showcasing: "The outreach group are consuming the potential customers and squandering our spending plan."

How would you qualify a prospective customer?

Typically, the 'amazing client' has a few critical qualities or properties that will impact their probability to purchase your item or administration.

A showcasing qualified lead (MQL) is a potential customer whose commitment levels propose that he is probably going to turn into a client.

As far as your site, this could be a guest who has shown interest in your site's substance. This could be the guest has finished up a web structure, have downloaded content, have pursued a bulletin or topped off the shopping basket and afterward left the website. Each kind of cooperation is relegated to a lead score, a metric that is expected to assist deals and showcasing staff with figuring out where the guest is in the purchasing cycle. Assuming the potential client is right off the bat in the purchasing cycle, it is typically the advertising division's responsibility to support the lead.

MQL contrasts to Sales Qualified Leads (SQL).

  SQLs frequently show quick interest in an organization's items or administrations, and a best practice is for a salesman to follow up on a SQL inside the initial 24 hours of disclosure This could be a client pursuing a preliminary of your foundation. MQLs, on the other hand, are leads of more broad interest that might require more training and follow-up to be changed over into deals that open doors.

How to portray the glow of prospective customers?

You will frequently hear the articulation Hot, Cold, Warm yet there are various understandings of what every one of these terms mean

Hot - Ready to purchase to satisfy a quick necessity. They have an accessible financial plan to finalize the negotiation.

Warm - Wish to buy, may have tested your item/administration. They may effectively be glancing near and contrasting specialist co-ops and elements, or might be gotten into another's agreement.

Cold - May never knew about you or could be searching for data that characterizes them as a lead, yet not prepared to purchase something now.

Top tips on the most proficient method to produce potential customers for your business.

1. Lead age organizations
In the event that you need more of the right potential customers in your CRM or data set today, you should dole out a spending plan to purchase potential customers. Contingent upon who you go to a portion of the primary issues with purchasing potential customers are: The information is old
You might be purchasing a lead that you as of now have in your CRM

You might be purchasing a lead that is as of now a client

You might be purchasing a lead that is against your AUP (Acceptable Use Policy).

Nonetheless, with the quick headways in innovation organizations are currently starting to beat these issues. Here is a rundown of lead age organizations:

SalesOptimize

Unomy

Hoovers

Insideview

DiscoverOrg

Found

Rainking

Datafox

2. Website optimization

Further develop the site improvement (SEO) of your site so you show up on the principal page of Google for watchwords that depict your item or administration. This will assist with directing people to your site and increment your inbound prospective customers. Attempt these SEO apparatuses first off:

Shouting Frog

Ahrefs

Google search console

Web optimization book

Hit Tail

Serpstat

3. Presentation pages

A presentation page is a page which a guest lands on for an unmistakable reason. While a presentation page can be utilized in light of multiple factors, one of its most regular purposes is to catch leads through utilization of structures, offers, preliminaries and so on. Simply a tip: It is better for you to house your greeting pages from outbound missions on your own waiter so the traffic goes to your site and not the facilitator's. In the event that you really do involve an outsider for presentation pages be careful that your missions assist with expanding their SEO positioning however won't benefit your own.

This is an interesting point while setting up presentation pages.

4. Online courses
Here the moderator is examining a subject pertinent to the business where his clients reside. This is commonly done utilizing slides or a meeting style show. Here is some great online class destinations:
Cisco WebEx
Webinato
ClickWebinar
GoToWebinar
BrightTalk

5. Websites
They are normally rich substances posted on a site as a post. Assuming your blog is great, you can request that different sites distribute your blog and along these lines create prospective customers and backlinks to your site.

6. Whitepapers

These are an incredible method for drawing in guests to your site or business. They are commonly a legitimate report or guide regarding a matter that is of interest to your future clients.

7. Catalogs
These are extremely valuable on the off chance that you are a B2B organization selling an item or administration. Numerous organizations acquire prospective customers as a result of promoting or basically being recorded in web-based catalogs. Here are a few instances of the more well known programming indexes:
G2Crowd
Capterra
GetApp
CabinetM
Programming Advice
SaaS Genius

8. Official statements
Giving official statements can assist with directing people to your site in this manner making inbound potential customers. Consider

the accompanying web-based official statement
destinations that offer a minimal expense
arrangement:
Cision
Business Wire
Marketwired
NewsWire
PR NewsWire

9. Client/worker/accomplice references
Set up a reference program where
workers/clients/accomplices can allude
prospective customers to your business.
Consider the accompanying programming
answers for make you ready rapidly;
Unbounce
Vocal References
Influitive
Welcome Referrals
InviteBox
Eve

10. Existing clients

Your current clients can be a mother lode for obtaining more prospective customers. Your deals or record supervisory crew will foster a relationship base on trust and can request acquaintances with your client's worldwide workplaces or merchants

Lead age is difficult however it is a priority cycle for any business to make due. A few organizations get by on inbound alone. Nonetheless, for the overwhelming majority B2B organizations and new companies this isn't a choice. I compare lead age to digging for gold. You ought to never rely exclusively upon one wellspring of leads yet have numerous hotspots for lead age in the event that one vein evaporates.

You really want to know the specific Niche to showcase your items to.

Numerous effective organizations rely upon adding to their client base to develop their business. One critical method for achieving this objective is to guarantee that organizations get a normal stream of deals leads. This is how you might create leads for your business.

Inbound showcasing techniques can assist your business with making a constant flow of inbound potential customers. Utilize the accompanying lead age techniques to create potential customers for your business.

1. Ask current clients for references.
Your ongoing clients can be your best wellspring of deals since they've proactively bought from you, so they know your items and administrations work. Subsequently, they ought to be a basic piece of your methodology to draw in new potential customers.

Warm references are more remarkable than cold messages or effort to possibilities who don't know anything about your business.

Be that as it may, numerous organizations don't get some margin to connect with current clients after the deal, past offering help or client assistance when inquired. They don't thank clients for their business nor do they request references or help with creating more business.

Following a portion of these systems can assist with transforming current clients into an incredible wellspring of deals leads:

Request that your record director guarantee that clients are happy with your items or administrations and client care. Have them contact track down ways of improving the circumstance.

Set up an opportunity to have a speedy discussion with your client, and say thanks to them for their business. Guarantee that they comprehend the amount you value their relationship and examine how you can enhance that relationship.

Request the names and contact data of business contacts or different organizations that could require your item or administration, as well as the motivations behind why they would make a solid match.

Request that your client contact the possibility for your sake, first through a short email or call. You can give them what to say in an email with the goal that the potential customer comprehends the worth you give.

Thank your client with a smart gift for the reference. Make it something individual as opposed to connected with the organization's items and administrations.

2. Work with your organization to recognize prospective customers.
Everybody has an individual organization of family, individual, and work companions, past and current business partners, neighbors, administration experts (e.g., handymen, specialists, legal counselors, greens keepers, etc.

You could disregard these individuals for various reasons as a wellspring of deals leads, but they ought to be one of your most memorable choices for doing as such. You as of now have their trust, which makes them important wellsprings of producing leads.

While the individuals from your organization share you practically speaking, a considerable lot of them exist in discrete parts of your life and don't cooperate with one another. They don't have similar contacts, so every individual can possibly give unimaginably important prospective customers. In the event that you've talked with them about existence and business, you can request that they associate you with possibilities.

How would you start the interaction? Just let them in on what you're looking for. Be explicit about the kind of individual or business you're hoping to interface with. Depict their industry, business size, deals and income ranges, geographic area, etc. On the off chance that they have an association, request that they connect for your benefit to make the presentation. Better actually, give them the email that they can forward to their contact.

Recall that you're managing a companion or colleague that you intend to keep as a feature of your organization. Blending your expert and individual lives implies you ought to be deferential of their time and the relationship.

3. Draw in with deals leads at systems administration occasions.
Make going to face to face and internet organizing occasions part of your daily schedule of finding prospective customers. Organizing is a viable method for contacting new individuals and assembling associations with individuals you've met before. It additionally permits you to connect with your leads up close and personal.

Organizing demands investment, so pick your occasions astutely. Go to systems administration occasions where your potential customers are probably going to prompt the best utilization of this time. Follow these techniques to capitalize on your systems administration:

Organizing includes building associations with genuine individuals. Try not to move toward individuals according to a deals viewpoint; all things considered, go in with the mentality of attempting to help others first. Learn about their business and about them as individuals, and distinguish what they need to succeed or take care of an issue.

For in-person organizing occasions, trade business cards with new individuals you meet. Add the individual's contact data to your client relationship with the executives framework. Follow up inside the week with an email to say thanks to them for meeting at the occasion.

For face to face and internet organizing occasions, inquire as to whether they might want to interface on LinkedIn. It's an extraordinary

method for keeping in contact, in any event,
when they move to another association.
Act naturally and have a great time.

4. Return to shut and lose open doors.
Here and there, "no" signifies "not at this
moment."

You've most likely connected with various
organizations that didn't buy from you around
then. Try to connect once more. They definitely
understand what your business does. You could
have shown your item or administration, and,
surprisingly, took part in a revelation call. They
didn't buy then, at that point, yet that could
change.

Return to shut or lost open doors. Reconnect
with the possibility each four to a half year.
Inquire as to whether anything has changed in
their business, like their needs, difficulties,
objectives and requirements.

Organizations that didn't buy from you before are now qualified prospective customers. Put time and assets into promoting these possibilities. Keep in contact through blog entries, customized correspondences and supported advertising messages.

You probably won't make the deal the following multiple times you contact them. Yet, you could get a deal or interest after the fourth, fifth or 6th time they hear from you. What's more, your possibility's circumstance will change. Their spending plan could increase to appear to be legit to buy your answer. Or on the other hand your contact could move to another organization or office, where there is a need or catalyst to carry out your answer.

Remaining top of mind with sales leads will make you the main business they call when it's the ideal opportunity for them to pick their deals arrangement.

5. Find potential customers on applicable web-based entertainment organizations. Everybody is web based, including your prospective customers. It's simply a question of finding and interfacing with them.

You're most likely on LinkedIn at the present moment (or ought to be), so use LinkedIn to create top-quality potential customers. Your most wanted associations and organizations in your specialty are on LinkedIn. They are here since they believe they should carry on with work, develop their organization, advance their items and administrations, and find answers for their business needs.

Follow these systems to utilize your virtual entertainment profile to produce new prospective customers:

Associate with whatever number of individuals in your current organization as could be expected under the circumstances, as well as deal leads and individuals in your industry. Each association assists with expanding your scope, as you can now interface with your contacts' associations. You don't have to know your associations by and by; any association can be a wellspring of extraordinary potential customers.

Tell your organization about your ideal possibilities and the sorts of issues you can assist them with addressing. You can compose a post or offer a report on the thing you're searching for at this moment. For instance: "We're hoping to assist dental specialists and orthodontists in the Denver region with extending their limited time reach during the class kickoff season."

Ask a few current clients to give proposals or tributes to the work you've accomplished for them to show your worth and client support. These methodologies are intended for LinkedIn. Notwithstanding, you can extend your organization's range and brand to other informal communities that fit your business, like Instagram, Facebook for Business, Twitter, Snapchat, etc. Pick the right online entertainment network for your business. Center your endeavors around web-based entertainment networks that will give the best prospective customers.

6. Upgrade your virtual entertainment profiles to draw in ideal potential customers.
In the event that you have a virtual entertainment profile, you want to stay up with the latest. Keeping your LinkedIn, Twitter, Instagram or other web-based entertainment profile current assists you with getting more prospective customers. The objective is to draw in the consideration of purchasers and make it simpler to associate.

LinkedIn: Create a strong title and depiction that will engage your interest group. Your title and rundown ought to depict what you do and who you serve. Center around what your objective purchaser will be searching for, utilizing catchphrases they would utilize. For instance, don't consider yourself a "Business Maven" - your title ought to express something like

"Project supervisor | Creating Solutions for Human Resources Managers in the Automotive Industry."

Twitter: notwithstanding your title and a connection to your organization's record, incorporate an expert profile photograph, a connection to your LinkedIn account and pertinent hashtags that would make a difference to your interest group. Follow Twitter profiles in your industry and those of potential prospective customers. Retweet and remark to keep your record dynamic.

Instagram: This virtual entertainment stage is extremely visual. Incorporate an expert photograph, as well as alluring and significant pictures, alongside hashtags that would make a difference to deals leads. Keep it proficient yet fun.

7. Make an email grouping.

An email succession is a progression of messages that are naturally shipped off gatherings in a mailing list. The objective is to utilize email promoting to construct beneficiaries' advantage in your organization's items or administrations.

There are two principal sorts of email arrangements:

Trigger-put together groupings send messages based with respect to the individual playing out a specific activity, like perusing a page on your site, purchasing an item, buying into your email rundown or leaving something unpurchased in a shopping basket.

Time sensitive groupings send messages at explicit times, for example, two weeks in the wake of making a buy, following picking in to get a pamphlet or a commemoration date.
To really draw in deals leads, email successions ought to be composed considering a particular reason. Each email in the arrangement expands on the past one to develop the peruser's advantage. For instance, you could follow this succession, where each email closes with a

source of inspiration (e.g., call for more data, click here to buy item):

First email: Introduce yourself and notice a typical trouble spot that your peruser may have.
Second email: Talk about the worth of your item or administration.
Third email: Discuss how a client tackled their concern with your item or administration.
Fourth email: Describe how you help clients.
Fifth email: Provide a rundown of advantages from utilizing your item or administration.
6th email: Reach out once again with an extraordinary deal.

8. Compose and distribute useful articles and online journals.
Composing a blog entry or article can assist with laying out you as a specialist in your field. Expound on what you know and how your insight can help other people. Subjects are perpetual, yet you could begin with how to help other people be more proficient, decrease costs,

increment deals, further develop efficiency, develop their business, etc.

Composing makes you a noticeable master. Individuals will actually want to peruse what you say, and see that you know your business. Your insight can instruct perusers, and when they need to know more or make a buy in light of what you've shown them, you'll be the one they go to.

Contributing to a blog is likewise essential for a substance showcasing methodology, which can direct people to your pages and assist with further developing your lead age endeavors. By involving content advertising as a component of your lead age methodology, you can support site traffic, driving your expected client to your planned presentation page.

On that greeting page, you can make a phone call to activity, which could urge a site guest to find out more, purchase now or take part in some other activity you believe potential leads should investigate

There are many spots to compose and distribute articles and blog entries:

Your own site or blog webpage
Your organization's site or blog page
LinkedIn and other virtual entertainment channels
Other corporate, industry and individual web journals
Sites that distribute industry online journals and articles
Your clients' sites
You can likewise make an email pamphlet to distribute sites and articles. This has the additional advantage of building associations with your interest group. Individuals need to join to get the pamphlet, so they are as of now inspired by what you need to say. They allow you to market to them, as long as you teach, illuminate or engage them en route.

9. Have an online class or online studio.
Articles and blog entries are perfect for sharing your insight and teaching individuals. Notwithstanding, they are one sided discussions - you compose and another person peruses. Online classes and online studios empower you to educate and collaborate with individuals, which can be more effective in making prospective customers.

Online courses and online studios permit you to go into more noteworthy profundity in offering your insight to possibilities. For instance, you could show individuals how to make a promoting effort in various advances, and use video and pictures to represent each step en route. Every individual who pursues the online class or studio is a real prospective customer. Offering your insight to individuals in this configuration lays out you as a forerunner in your field, constructs trust and expands your capacity to draw in leads.

You can run live online classes and online studios so you can address inquiries continuously and make time-restricted live proposals to connect with deals leads. You can likewise record online courses and studios to contact individuals 24 hours every day, and draw in deals leads in any event, when you are not there. You can have online courses and online studios on your organization's site, or make and host them on destinations that distribute online courses.

10. Interface with live talk clients.
Talk innovation has made considerable progress, on account of man-made consciousness and AI. You can make a customized chatbot for your site that matches your corporate image's look and feel. Any time somebody visits your site, the chatbot can show up on their screen with a welcome message.

A chatbot can do significantly more than say "hi." It can turn into an important expansion to your deals and promoting groups. A chatbot can:

Get clarification on pressing issues and give reactions that address the requirements of the prospective customers

Qualify potential customers

Book arrangements and gatherings

Answer usually clarified some things

Associate guests to the right contact

You can likewise survey the discussions between the chatbot and potential customer to look further into the client and see where you can add esteem, draw in with the prospective customer and work on your chatbot's reactions. Everything relies upon the abilities of the chatbot programming, and how you want it to help you.

What are the Skills you really want to produce deals?

A key to effectively sharing and selling an item, administration or thought, is to seek clarification on pressing issues and afterward listen discreetly and cautiously to the responses. A considerable lot of us make a solid attempt to persuade individuals to purchase as opposed to finding what our future client or client truly needs, needs and wants from us.

To prevail in deals recollect these three tuning in and relationship building abilities:

- **S - Sincerity** - Listen without a plan, it's not necessary to focus on your requirements.

- **E - Ethics** - Don't attempt to talk somebody into something, stand by listening to what they need.

- **A - Asking** - Serve others by posing inquiries that will help them in going with a savvy purchasing choice.

Building shared benefit connections implies recalling that there's no need to focus on what we need yet what the other individual needs. The following are three relationship building abilities that when utilized routinely will make them increment deals and make fulfilled faithful clients.

1. Listening genuinely and without a plan. The purchasing system isn't about you and your needs and needs, it is about the client. An excessive number of us come to the deals table with our own plan. We are once in a while too bustling pondering standards, advancements and commissions. There's actually no need to focus on us, it's about the needs, necessities and assumptions for the planned purchaser.

A salesman with a plan will in general push excessively hard and frequently doesn't listen well. Leave your plan at home. Earnestly center around your client and how your item can best serve their expectations, dreams and objectives. Zig Ziglar said all that needed to be said, "You can have everything in life that you need on the off chance that you simply give an adequate number of others what they need."

2. Try not to talk somebody into something,
permit them to settle on their own purchasing
choice. Making the right decision for everybody
in question is the moral thing to do. I'm helped
to remember an expression from Dale Carnegie's
book, How To Win Friends and Influence
People, "A man persuaded despite his desire to
the contrary is of a similar assessment still."

Your part in the deals cycle is to introduce your
item in an unmistakable, compact and honest
way — with uprightness. The best client is the
client who can go with an informed choice in
light of what is best for them. An unwavering
client is an informed client. You are not in the
persuading industry, you are in the sharing
industry. Your responsibility is to morally offer
the item, administration or thought, make sense
of the advantages and answer questions. Your
client or client will then pursue a purchasing
choice in light of the data they've been given.
Making the deal is tied in with clarifying some
things, responding to questions and building a
dependable mutually beneficial relationship.

3. You can serve your client/client best by figuring out what they need, need and anticipate from what you are advertising. Here and there, we are so eager to share all that we realize about the thing we're offering that we fail to remember it is about your likely client's assumptions. What is vital to you may not mean quite a bit to them.

I'm helped to remember a story: A youthful mother simply beginning with an enormous organization showcasing organization was energized and anxious to impart her business to other housewives. She was having espresso with a possible enlist as their kids played close by. The youthful mother was enthusiastically showing her items and making sense of the business potential. She continued endlessly about how she could remain at home with her youngsters and didn't need to take off from the house to lead business.

The mother who was listening appeared to switch off her advantage and consideration abruptly. At the point when our enthusiastic youthful organization showcasing mother requested that her companion join her in the business, the companion answered with a resonating, "No," The business-building mother was stunned and disheartened, "Why?" she inquired. "Since," her companion said, "I need to have the option to do something that permits me to escape the house and associate with different grown-ups."

Lesson of the story: Ask questions and tune in. Try not to expect that what is critical to you means a lot to your future clients.

Effective selling isn't about what you need, it is about how you might best serve the requirements of your clients and clients. Coming from a true spot of administration, will assist with expanding deals and foster faithful client and reference base.

Keeping the three components of SEA (Sincerity, Ethics, Asking) as a main priority, you can undoubtedly and easily find new clients and clients who you believe should work with you now and later on. Selling your administration, item or thought is tied in with making the best decision for all interested parties - it is tied in with building a win-to-win relationship.

In the following part you will know how to duplicate your deals to push up your pay.

Chapter 3

How to multiply your sales?

Duplicating your sales depends on two viewpoints. These perspectives are you and your possibilities. You are vital to calculate your business and your deals since you pick the manner in which you model your deals and you pick the manner in which you draw in and respond to your clients.

The most effective method to Deal With Yourself In Sales Making
By setting norms :
Now that you probably known your designated crowd, have made an incentive and constructed areas of strength for a, the main step turns into the standard setting and documentation, all things considered,
  A deals cycle record is complete, and you ought to incorporate outlined, higher perspectives of each step en route. From

dispersion channels, suspicion approvals, progress measurements, and deals pipes — all become the structure blocks you gather. All the more significantly, your work process is the spot to track all thoughts.

Besides the fact that this makes any blemishes simpler to perceive and fix, yet it likewise makes everybody's work more straightforward over the long haul. The manner in which you coordinate your deals technique assumes a major part in staying with the development diagram pointing north and getting steady benefits each term.

Put forth **SMART** objectives to adjust deals and showcasing.
Laying out an objective is the initial step to accomplishing it. For your deals and advertising groups, SMART objectives ought to be the ideal to take a stab at. Brilliant brand objectives go further into the particulars of what your image expects to achieve. The object is to add tone to the objective with unambiguous subtleties and outline a way to accomplish it.

Your objectives ought to follow the exemplary deals rule, **SMART**:

Specific: Increase client lifetime esteem is explicit and huge for long haul development.

Measurable: Improve benefits by X% in 2021-22 monetary year

Achievable: Increase normal client lifetime esteem by X%

Relevant: Improve benefits in the monetary year to acquire a piece of the pie in the business.

Time based: Increase normal client lifetime esteem by X% in the following Y years.

Recognize any bottlenecks through criticism you get, and find approaches to upkeep clear correspondence among all groups to guarantee least conceivable efficiency slacks. By killing all uncertainty from your ultimate objective, you can successfully provide your group with the bedrock of a substantial objective.

KEEP YOUR FUNNEL FULL.

You can not find business visionaries that don't need their "deals channel" to continuously be full. Deals pipe is the course of offer and development of your likely clients between various levels until they become purchasers.

On the off chance that you as a business person prevail with regards to making your pipe in every case full, your business won't have issues connected with powerless deals or lacking new cash for business purposes.

You might be thinking whether your business pipe can be in a "Respite" Mode?
   " **NO**"
The deals channel isn't something that can quit working or be in a "stop" mode. At the point when the pipe becomes in such a position, then, at that point, your business is in huge issues.

Your business deals pipe is like the genuine channel which effectively moves fluid from a more extensive tank into a container that has a slim opening. You add fluid in the more extensive finish of the pipe, while on the more slender side leave a similar fluid and enter the jug. All the more critically, the channel is utilized not to permit your fluid to become squander that didn't go straightforwardly into the container. On the off chance that you quit adding the fluid to the more extensive side of the channel, then the pipe "evaporates," and the entire cycle will wrap up.

A deals channel is accustomed to carry expected clients into the more extensive side of the pipe, who know about your item or administration. In any case, assuming on the more extensive side stop the section of expected clients, your business pipe will evaporate, and separately on the more slender side won't come purchasers.

Hence, the business pipe ought to constantly be full, and your occupation as a business person and your workers is all to guarantee that the business channel will continuously be full.

How Might You Make Your Sales Funnel Always Full?
The accompanying exercises can give your business channel to be in every case full:

1. Reinforcing the Marketing Activities toward the Beginning Point of the Funnel
Here, reinforcement doesn't mean spending more cash on various promoting exercises. Basically, this implies more astute use and the mix of showcasing devices that truly bring great outcomes.

2. Ceaseless Improvement of Marketing Activities
Ceaseless improvement is a cycle that a business visionary ought to always remember. Everything can be improved, thus any showcasing exercises and missions of your business can be improved too.

You want to test all that you do as a piece of your promoting endeavors. This will bring consistent improvement that will empower more powerful showcasing processes in your organization.

3. Consistent Improvement of the Sales Processes

Again an improvement. Where advertising closes is where deals start. Through advertising, you as a business visionary prevail to stand out to your business and your items and administrations, yet the genuine choice about buying will depend on your outreach group.

In this way, essentially execute solid deals cycles and begin utilizing trials to test and see what produces the best outcomes, and what should be taken out or worked on all the while.

4) Customer Satisfaction

This is a vital element for any business. On the off chance that you have another item or administration, you can undoubtedly offer to somebody who as of now has a decent involvement in your business. Thus, a fulfilled client will constantly be important for your deals channel. You should produce however much as could reasonably be expected of more fulfilled clients toward the finish of the channel in the event that you maintain that they should proceed with the business with you.

You should produce however much as could reasonably be expected of more fulfilled clients toward the finish of the pipe in the event that you maintain that they should proceed with the business with you.

Increment realizing exposure with your clients and conquer dread of dismissal.
Try not to constantly get to your clients through telephone or on the web. You can in some cases attempt to see them eye to eye and discuss your items and different things ala productive to them. Try not to fear being dismissed on the grounds that people contrast and some will most

likely oddball and some will acknowledge you.
It is to fear.

Master different deals abilities.

Manage Your Customer In Sales Making.
  After effectively managing yourself, the
following thing is your client. The manner in
which you treat your clients are vital and basic to
your business.
  These are fruitful tips on how you really want
to manage your clients.

1. Pay attention to Customers and acknowledge
them how they are.
Here and there, clients simply have to realize
that you're tuning in. Assuming that they're
confused or have an issue, by listening closely,
you're showing that you give it a second thought
and that you're not excusing them.

2. Apologize
When something turns out badly, apologize. It's
astounding how quieting the words "Please

accept my apologies" can be. Try not to take part in issue finding or laying fault, however let them in on you're sorry they had an issue. Manage the issue right away and let the client in on what you have done.

3. Treat Them In a serious way
Cause clients to feel significant and appreciated. Regardless of how crazy an inquiry might sound to you; it means a lot to the client. In the event that they feel like they're being snickered at, or spoken down to, they won't buy anything. Clients can be extremely touchy and will know whether you truly care about them.

4. Remain cool-headed
Troublesome as it is at times, remaining mentally collected is significant. Your quieting approach will assist your client with keeping mentally collected as well. They will feel like you're in charge of the circumstance and that you can assist with tackling their concern.

5. Recognize and Anticipate Needs

Most client needs are personal as opposed to intelligent. The more you know your clients, the better you become at expecting their necessities. Impart routinely so that you're mindful of issues or impending requirements.

6. Recommend Solutions
Have a menu of quieting cures which you and your workers can utilize. Whether it's simply a discount or return, or on the other hand on the off chance that it's coupons or a free help. By concurring ahead of time the situations where you will give these cures, and the amount you're willing to spend, you will actually want to talk more quiet and all the more without hesitation while offering the arrangement.

7. Value the Power of "Yes"
Continuously search for ways of aiding your clients. At the point when they have a solicitation (for however long it is sensible) let them know that you can make it happen. Sort out how subsequently. Search for ways of making

working with you simple. Continuously do what you say you will do.

8. Recognize Your Limits

Indeed is a strong word yet in the event that you can't satisfy a solicitation: know your cutoff points. You can't be everything to everybody. On the off chance that you don't figure you can satisfy the solicitation, assist them with tracking down a substitute cure. Whether that cure is your business or another, they will see the value in the additional mile you went to help them, and will prescribe your business to their organization.

9. Be Available

Client support is at this point not just turn around to-confront contact and phone. Assuming you're working in an industry or commercial center where clients are continually on the web, you really want to change your administration conveyance to consolidate that.

10. Get Regular Feedback

Input is an incredible method for developing
both your business and your abilities. Give
approaches to clients to give criticism, whether
it's a subsequent email or call, an ideas box or
something more tomfoolery and inventive.

Chapter 4

SALES MANAGEMENT.

What sales management?
Sales management is the most common way of creating, arranging, observing, and controlling the whole course of selling your organization's labor and products. It additionally concerns enlisting, preparing, and administering your business power and covers all pre-deals, deals, and post-deals exercises.

Sales Management ;
This remains on three points:

1. Procedure
Without having a reasonable methodology your business endeavors will be pointless. To understand assets' and experts' expectations, you ought to set up a business interaction and plan a progression of exercises at each phase of your business channel or deals pipeline. This should

be possible for either the entire organization or concerning individual brands, merchandise, or administrations.

A deals pipe is a strong scientific device, whenever planned with an information first methodology. It depicts a solitary client's excursion through 5 stages: mindfulness, interest, thought, choice, and — the most wanted stage for all organizations — buy.

The channel conditions deal with the pipeline — decided phases of contacting clients. It changes between organizations, contingent upon the market type, assets possessed, and business targets. In any case, when in doubt, the pipeline has such stages as lead age, capability, meeting, proposition, and settling the negotiation.

Remembering the channel and the pipeline, you'll have the option to think of a reported deals plan. This commonly covers:

Advancement objectives

Deals KPIs
Purchaser personas profiles
Individuals and cycles
Precise selling approaches
Programming required.

2. **Activities**

A complex system is good for nothing without being carried out. You really want the group on paper to work out as expected. Individuals are the hindrance that isolates normal organizations from the best players on the lookout.

It's not just that agents bring you income — they are your image's ministers. Salesmen straightforwardly manage:

Lead transformation. They fabricate an extension between what the client needs and what your organization can offer.
Business development. Agents instate references and assist with building client steadfastness.
Client maintenance. Their associations with clients ought not be under-assessed. Recollect

that a 5% increment in standards for dependability might help benefits by 25%.

3. Examination

Deals examination concerns either KPIs and deals measurements. A central issue here is to bring noteworthy experiences that can be additionally utilized in the deals technique. The accompanying adequacy pointers are typically utilized by most team leads:

Absolute income
Income development rate
Income conveyance by sources
Income conveyance by delegates
Normal change rate
Deals to-date
Normal buy esteem.
Deals the board interaction
Despite the fact that all colleagues add to business objectives, it's the administrator's liability to take care of business. Their assignments include:

1. Laying out objectives
To deal with the interaction, you really want to
have a deals guide. With it, it's feasible to follow
the reps' continuous exhibition and opportunely
decide if thorough help is expected to
accomplish the objectives.

2. Arranging and overseeing deals exercises
This area of obligation concerns creating and
testing deals exercises. Evaluating new advances
and approaches is the main way your group can
prevail with regards to supporting clients better
than contenders do.

3. Spurring the group
Assuming that you fabricate colleagues' abilities,
you'll support worker maintenance and
increment representative lifetime. Try not to turn
out to be excessively trial, nonetheless. Utilize
past techniques for worker maintenance — the
ones that have been tried by ages of chiefs:

Put forth **SMART** objectives as I have
composed above . An endless quest for out of

reach results is debilitating and prompts profound and proficient burnout.

Value individual commitment. Gen Z are not the ones who will hang tight for changes — they need to lead them. Assuming your esteem ability, be prepared to give them adequate room for drive and independent direction.

Assemble trust. Let each colleague appreciate the situation and go over plans with your kin. Share development hacking experiences, corporate key objectives, and how the organization's doing in general. On the off chance that there are a few issues — convey these.

Empower superior execution culture. Develop an outcomes based workplace approach instead of only a work-to-take care of business approach.

4. Assessing and announcing

For each choice you make or understanding you talk, put numbers in front. Utilize fundamental programming, make deals dashboards, and convey thorough business numbers. Make

information incorporated and envision where it
is important.

Deals the board programming model.
Involving mechanization in your business
revealing will forestall:

Income error
Unfortunate information access
Leaders being over-burden with superfluous and
obsolete data.
Viable deals the executives strategies
The fact that brings you results makes the best
strategy. Whichever you embrace, ensure it
doesn't seem like "Increment deals by 500% the
following month." Just don't. Numbers can't be a
strategy. A fourth of organizations couldn't
actually say whether their salesforce
accomplishes that standard.

All things considered, center around joining
administrative accepted procedures and concoct
something that will help your income:

1. Track down the ideal individuals

Obviously, staffing is an obligation of the HR division. Yet, for the administrator, it's urgent to make an interpretation of vision and necessities to future representatives to employ the perfect individuals.

However, the "right" doesn't actually imply "the best. Try not to search for Jack, all things considered. Over-burden sets of responsibilities are not viable. Characterize 2 or 3 central issues that are applicable and go on hunting future agents.

2. Keep away from "one-size-fits-all" choices

Anything you make due, individuals or cycles, stay away from distortion and an excess of extrapolation. What works in an emergency may not work when the development starts, as well as the other way around. Be adaptable and an out-of-the-crate mastermind.

3. Recruit experts for various jobs

On the off chance that your business develops, you'll need to partition liabilities. One representative can't join a few jobs. When you feel your laborers can't adapt to how much work and undertakings they get — employ more experts.

4. Add to the development of every agent

Best sales reps bring your organization the most arrangements because of their experience, individual characteristics, karma, or every one of the three all at once. Be that as it may, assuming that the group's irregularity develops quickly, you get a ton of conceded gambles:

Internal pressure
Loss of inspiration
Indispensable workers.
The supervisor's undertaking here is to comprehend the reason why one agent performs far superior to other people and settle what is going on. This isn't tied in with adjusting all, this is tied in with tracking down places of development for each colleague.

Wrapping up

Outreach group achievement generally decides your organization's general exhibition in light of the fact that these folks acquire the income. Focus that the methodology and strategies utilized are adequately applicable to accomplish business targets.

Conclusion

Sales is a developing yet underestimated administration discipline. Looking at this logically: There are a lot of "how to… " approaches out there. These counselors are valuable yet principally divided and independent arrangements. A significant inquiry that you ought to continuously pose to yourself is: How do these selling approaches fit into your organization's business theory? Consolidating the miniature and large scale viewpoint of this book is hence essential. This book is a worthy driver to get consistent deals development. So in the wake of perusing this book, you ought to have a decent comprehension of the deals cycle, deals climate, outreach group and the deals driven business the executives approach to be prepared for prompt and enduring deals achievement. Regardless of the off chance that you fill in as a deals chief, salesman, deals engineer, business visionary, proprietor, or director or in deals related positions. In the end everybody sells, or needs to sell at certain places throughout everyday life.

Being a conceited salesperson isn't fundamental. Truth be told, the larger part of fruitful sales reps across most business sectors have been made through their own assurance and advancement.